WRAYDAWN SHEND

Survivors Rise: Unveiling the Truth Behind Injustice

Contents

Outline

1. This chapter explores the resilience and strength of survivors, highlighting their journey towards healing and empowerment.

2. An examination of the various forms of injustice survivors face, including systemic oppression and societal barriers.

3. Explores the importance of survivors sharing their stories and the impact it has on raising awareness and promoting change.

4. An in-depth look at the key role advocacy groups play in fighting for survivor rights and dismantling systems of injustice.

5. Examining the effects of trauma on survivors mental and emotional well-being, and strategies for healing and recovery.

6. An exploration of how intersecting identities, such as race, gender, class, and sexuality, can compound the injustices survivors face and the need for inclusive advocacy.

7. An overview of the legal challenges survivors encounter when seeking justice, including the importance of legal reforms

and support.

8. Highlighting the power of collective action and community support in creating healing spaces for survivors.

9. An exploration of the truth behind some high-profile cases of injustice and how survivor's stories brought the truth to light.

10. A rallying call for individuals, communities, and institutions to support survivors and work towards a just and equitable society.

Introduction

The Power of Survivors

In a world filled with adversity, injustice, and countless obstacles, there exists a group of individuals who possess an unparalleled strength and resilience. These are the survivors, the brave souls who have endured unimaginable pain and suffering, yet managed to rise above their circumstances and find solace in their journey towards healing and empowerment.

Each survivor's story is unique, shaped by the intensity of their experiences and the profound impact it has had on their lives. From survivors of abuse to those who have battled life-threatening illnesses, their stories are both heart-wrenching and inspiring. In this chapter, we delve into the depths of their struggles and triumphs, shedding light on their incredible power to overcome and thrive.

One of the most remarkable aspects of survivors is their unwavering determination in the face of adversity. Despite the trauma they have endured, they refuse to let it define them. Instead, they channel their pain into a catalyst for change and growth. Through their personal journeys, they have discovered the strength within themselves to rise above their past and embrace a future filled with hope and possibility.

The path towards healing is not without its challenges. Survivors often face a long and arduous journey, constantly navigating the ups and downs, as they navigate through the stages of grief and come to terms with their experiences. It is an ongoing process, marked by moments of triumph and setbacks. Yet, it is through this process that survivors find their inner strength and become warriors of their own lives.

In the face of injustice, survivors rise as advocates for change. They refuse to be silenced and instead use their voices to shed light on the dark corners of society. They rally together, forming support networks and advocacy groups to fight for justice, raise awareness, and ensure that others do not suffer the same fate. Their resilience becomes a powerful force, shining a light on the truth behind injustice and igniting a spark of hope in the hearts of so many.

The stories of survivors are not only a testament to their own strength but serve as a beacon of hope for others who find themselves in similar situations. Through sharing their experiences, survivors provide reassurance that healing is possible and that they are not alone. They inspire others to find the strength within themselves to rise above their circumstances and take control of their own narratives.

As we dive deeper into the journeys of survivors, we discover the transformative power of self-empowerment. By reclaiming their power, survivors break free from the chains of their past and unlock their full potential. They cultivate self-love, rebuild their shattered confidence, and emerge as warriors, ready to embrace life with open arms.

The power of survivors extends far beyond their individual stories; it reverberates across communities, societies, and generations. Their resilience becomes a catalyst for change, inspiring others to take action and challenge the status quo. Survivors remind us of the strength of the human spirit and the capacity for growth and healing even in the face of unimaginable adversity.

In the realm of survival, there is an unspoken bond that connects each individual. It transcends geographical borders and cultural differences, uniting survivors and advocacy groups around the world. Together, they form a collective force, determined to bring about positive change and create a world where justice and healing prevail.

As we explore the power of survivors, we embark on a journey of self-discovery, empathy, and resilience. In the second half of this chapter, we will delve into the transformative processes survivors undergo on their path to healing and empowerment. Their stories will leave you in awe and ignite a fire within your soul, urging you to rise alongside them. But that is a story for another time, as we move forward with their extraordinary narratives, propelled by the strength and resilience that lie within each survivor.In the second half of this chapter, we delve deeper into the transformative processes survivors undergo on their path to healing and empowerment. Their stories, filled with resilience and determination, will leave you in awe and ignite a fire within your soul, urging you to rise alongside them.

Survivors embark on a journey of self-discovery and self-care, recognizing the importance of investing time and energy into their well-being. Through therapy, support groups, and various healing modalities, they learn to cope with and process their traumatic experiences. By facing their pain head-on and working through their emotions, survivors reclaim their power and find a newfound sense of peace.

During this healing process, survivors often encounter moments of self-doubt and fear. They question their worthiness and find themselves grappling with the lingering effects of their trauma. However, with the support of their networks and the strength they have cultivated over time, survivors learn to push past these obstacles. They gradually rebuild their shattered confidence and understand their inherent value and strength.

As survivors continue on their journey, they begin to cultivate self-love and self-compassion. They recognize that their worthiness is not determined by the actions of their perpetrators or the injustices they have faced. Survivors learn to embrace their scars as badges of resilience and write their own narratives, free from the constraints of their past. In doing so, they create space for growth, acceptance, and transformation.

Throughout their healing process, survivors also develop a deep sense of empathy and compassion for others who have endured similar traumas. They understand the importance of providing support and a safe space for fellow survivors to heal and grow. Whether through peer mentoring, advocacy work, or simply offering a listening ear, survivors become beacons of hope for others who are still navigating the complexities of their own healing journeys.

Survivors rise not only for themselves but also for future generations. They recognize the significance of breaking the cycle of abuse and creating a world where justice and healing prevail. By raising awareness, pushing for legal reforms, and challenging societal norms, survivors become agents of change. Their collective voice becomes a powerful force that resonates across communities and inspires others to join the fight against injustice.

In the face of adversity, survivors refuse to be defined by their past. They choose to rise, to create a future that is free from the chains of trauma and injustice. Their resilience and strength serve as a guiding light for others who may be struggling in the darkness. Survivors show us that healing is possible, that there is power in our stories, and that we can overcome even the darkest of circumstances.

As we come to the end of this chapter, we are reminded of the incredible power that resides within survivors. Their journey towards healing and empowerment is a testament to the indomitable spirit of the human soul. They stand as living proof that with resilience, support, and unwavering determination, we can rise above the depths of despair and reclaim our lives.

To all the survivors and advocacy groups out there, your strength, courage, and unwavering spirit inspire us all. May your stories continue to ignite change, empower others, and bring forth a world where justice and healing prevail.

Unmasking Injustice

An examination of the various forms of injustice survivors face, including systemic oppression and societal barriers.

In a world marked by constant struggle, survivors emerge as beacons of strength and resilience, battling against the injustices that have plagued their lives. The journey of a survivor is one of immense courage, navigating through a myriad of challenges to reclaim their lives and seek truth and justice. This chapter delves deep into the multifaceted nature of injustices survivors face, shedding light on the systemic oppression and societal barriers that loom heavily over their path to healing.

Systemic oppression, often rooted in deeply ingrained power structures, casts a long shadow over the lives of survivors. Institutions, such as law enforcement agencies or judicial systems, can perpetuate and exacerbate the very injustices they are meant to combat. The systematic biases embedded within these institutions can hinder survivors from receiving the support and justice they rightfully deserve. Discrimination based on race, gender, socioeconomic status, and other intersecting identities can further compound the challenges faced by survivors.

For survivors of sexual assault, the journey to justice can be fraught with additional obstacles. Society often demands that survivors prove their credibility and confronts them with victim-blaming narratives. This undue burden on the survivor perpetuates a culture of silence and further erodes their sense of agency. The plea for justice is often met with skepticism, disbelief, and the devaluation of survivor testimonies. Such systemic failures reinforce the power dynamics and form barriers that survivors must confront as they navigate the legal labyrinth in search of justice.

Moreover, survivors face societal barriers that impede their healing and reintegration into everyday life. Isolation and social stigma often form an insurmountable wall, further deepening the wounds inflicted by injustice. The prevailing societal narratives may perpetuate victim-blaming attitudes, causing survivors to feel misunderstood, judged, and invalidated. This external pressure complicates their journey towards healing, eroding trust in themselves and others.

Societal expectations and norms can also hinder survivors from accessing vital resources and support networks. A survivor may be forced into a constant cycle of reliving their trauma, as insensitive inquiries and unhelpful interventions disregard their boundaries and hinder their healing process. Additionally, survivors may struggle to find secure housing, employment, or education due to prejudices and preconceived judgments held by others. These obstacles, rooted in societal biases, limit survivors' opportunities for growth and recovery.

The battle against injustice faced by survivors is far from over. It requires collective understanding, support, and proactive efforts to dismantle the oppressive systems that perpetuate their suffering. Advocacy groups play a pivotal role in empowering survivors, helping them navigate through the complex web of injustice. These organizations formulate strategies, raise awareness, and lobby for legislative changes to address the systemic failures that survivors endure.

In the second half of this chapter, we will explore the resilience of survivors in the face of adversity and delve into the transformative potential of collective action. Together, survivors and advocacy groups are paving the way towards a more just and inclusive society.The resilience of survivors shines brightly amidst the darkness of adversity, as they strive not only for personal healing but also for a broader societal transformation. Harnessing the power of collective action, survivors and advocacy groups are uniting to bring about tangible change and dismantle the oppressive systems perpetuating their suffering.

Survivors who have experienced injustice are no longer content with merely surviving; they are reclaiming their voice and demanding justice. Through the support and guidance of advocacy groups, survivors are finding the strength to navigate the unfamiliar terrain of legal processes and societal barriers. These organizations provide survivors with guidance, resources, and a platform to share their stories, fostering a sense of empowerment and solidarity.

One crucial aspect of collective action is the power of survivor storytelling. Countless survivors have broken their silence, courageously sharing their experiences with the world. By amplifying survivors' voices, advocacy groups are challenging the prevailing victim-blaming narratives and dispelling myths surrounding injustice. These narratives create a deep impact, leading to increased awareness and empathy within society.

Moreover, advocacy groups play a vital role in raising public consciousness about the systemic failures survivors face. By organizing awareness campaigns, they shed light on the flaws within institutions, demanding accountability and equitable treatment for survivors. These efforts force society to confront its biases and take a critical look at the pervasive nature of injustice.

Legislative changes are another significant aspect of the collective action undertaken by survivors and advocacy groups. Through policy advocacy, these groups actively engage with lawmakers to push for reforms that address the systemic failures perpetuating injustice. They work towards the creation of survivor-centered legislation, supporting survivors' rights and ensuring access to resources and support networks.

Furthermore, survivors and advocacy groups collaborate to build safe spaces where survivors can heal and find support. These spaces, both physical and virtual, provide solace, understanding, and opportunities for survivors to connect with others who have faced similar challenges. Sharing experiences, exchanging coping strategies, and collectively envisioning a future free from injustice, survivors find solace in these communities of support.

In the face of adversity, survivors demonstrate incredible strength, resilience, and determination. They refuse to be defined solely by their experiences of injustice but rather chart their own path towards healing and personal growth. They actively seek out opportunities for self-empowerment, engaging in therapeutic practices, education, and personal development.

Survivors, armed with newfound strength, often become advocates themselves. With an intimate understanding of the complexities and barriers associated with injustice, survivors are uniquely positioned to be powerful agents of change. They lend their voices to the advocacy movement, sharing their stories, and inspiring others to rise above their circumstances.

Survivors and advocacy groups are united by the common goal of dismantling oppressive systems and striving towards a more just and inclusive society. Together, they work tirelessly to challenge societal norms, combat victim-blaming attitudes, and create sustainable change. Their collective efforts remind us that the fight against injustice is ongoing and require the continued support and collaboration of individuals and communities alike.

As survivors rise and join forces with advocacy groups, they embody a beacon of hope, illuminating the path towards a future where justice, empathy, and equality prevail. Their journey is a testament to the indomitable human spirit, reminding us that through solidarity and collective action, we can dismantle the very systems that perpetuate injustice and embrace a world where survivors can heal, grow, and thrive.

Speaking Their Truth

I n the realm of justice, the power of survivors' stories cannot be underestimated. By sharing their experiences and revealing the painful truths behind injustices, survivors play a vital role in raising awareness and effecting positive change. Their voices have the capacity to penetrate the veil of ignorance and indifference, compelling society to confront uncomfortable realities and strive for a future where injustice is no longer tolerated.

Survivors, in their narratives, offer an unfiltered glimpse into the world of injustice. Their stories elucidate the multifaceted nature of the struggles they have endured, exposing the underlying systems that perpetuate inequality and discrimination. Through their honesty and vulnerability, survivors unveil the truth that can no longer be hidden or denied. It is through their truth that a collective understanding of the magnitude and urgency of the issue is fostered.

The act of sharing their stories can be both liberating and healing for survivors. It allows them to break the chains of silence and stigma that often bind them, enabling them to reclaim their identity and find solace in the solidarity of others who have walked similar paths. By lending their voices to the cause, survivors become catalysts for change, inspiring others to come forward and prompting society to recognize and address the systemic failures that perpetuate injustice.

Moreover, survivors' stories serve as catalysts for awareness and empathy. The power of personal narratives lies in their ability to bridge the gap between statistics and human experience. Numbers can be numbing, but stories offer a visceral connection that humanizes the issue at hand. Survivors' stories humanize the statistics, making them impossible to ignore or dismiss. They stir emotions, provoke introspection, and spur action from all those who bear witness to their truth.

Furthermore, survivors' stories have the potential to dismantle societal prejudices and challenge deeply ingrained biases. By articulating the realities they have faced, survivors expose the fallacies and misconceptions that often surround issues of injustice. By unmasking these preconceived notions, survivors prompt society to question its assumptions and reevaluate its beliefs.

Survivors' stories also hold immense power in the realm of policy change. When their experiences are shared, policymakers are confronted with a stark reminder of the urgency to rectify the systemic failures that perpetuate injustice. The human faces behind the statistics demand action. Survivors' stories, when paired with rigorous data and research, form a formidable force that compels lawmakers to reevaluate existing laws, address loopholes, and legislate for a just and equitable society.

The impact of survivors sharing their stories is immeasurable, both on an individual and societal level. By speaking their truth, survivors ignite a ripple effect that extends far beyond their immediate circle. They empower others to join the fight against injustice, foster alliances with advocacy groups, and provide inspiration and hope to those who might feel trapped and voiceless.

Before we delve further into the far-reaching consequences of survivors sharing their stories, we must acknowledge the challenges survivors face in doing so. The process of disclosing painful experiences can be emotionally and psychologically demanding. However, the benefits that arise from sharing their truth are profound. In the following chapters, we will explore the nuances of survivors' narratives, the challenges they navigate, and the transformative impact their stories have on society.

With survivors as beacons of resilience and courage, this chapter aims to shed light on the undeniable significance of speaking their truth. As we listen to the stories of survivors, their voices resound with a call for justice, pushing us closer to a world where injustice has no place and the truth is a weapon that will never be silenced.

Within the tapestry of survivors' narratives lies the power to dismantle oppressive systems and foster lasting change. By sharing their truth, survivors initiate a ripple effect that extends far beyond their immediate circle, igniting a spark of resilience and courage within others. Advocacy groups and society at large have a critical role to play in recognizing, amplifying, and honoring survivors' stories.

One of the key roles of advocacy groups is to provide a safe and supportive space for survivors to come forward and share their experiences. By offering resources, counseling, and legal support, these groups help survivors navigate the emotionally and psychologically demanding process of disclosure. They instill survivors with a sense of solidarity, reminding them that they are not alone in their journey. Through these connections, advocacy groups foster resilience and empower survivors to reclaim their voice.

Advocacy groups also play a pivotal role in amplifying survivors' voices through various channels. By utilizing their networks and platforms, these groups ensure that survivors' stories can reach a wider audience. They collaborate with media outlets, organize awareness campaigns, and host events that center survivors' narratives. In doing so, they elevate the visibility of survivors' experiences, strengthen public awareness, and challenge societal indifference towards injustice.

Furthermore, advocacy groups act as allies, standing beside survivors in their fight for justice. They work tirelessly to ensure that survivors' narratives are listened to, believed, and taken seriously. Through their efforts, they push for systemic changes that address the root causes of injustice. By advocating for policy reforms, raising public awareness, and holding institutions accountable, these groups help create an environment where survivors' stories can prompt tangible change.

In order to be effective allies, it is crucial for advocacy groups to approach survivors' stories with respect, sensitivity, and cultural humility. Each survivor's experience is unique, influenced by factors such as race, gender, sexuality, and socioeconomic background. Acknowledging this intersectionality is essential to providing comprehensive support and promoting inclusivity within the advocacy community. Respectful collaboration ensures that the voices of marginalized survivors are uplifted and that their experiences are acknowledged and validated.

Survivors themselves also have a vital role to play in shaping the narratives that surround injustice. By speaking their truth, survivors challenge societal norms, debunk stereotypes, and directly confront the deeply ingrained biases that perpetuate injustice. They disrupt the dominant narratives that seek to silence their voices and instead assert their own agency and power.

In sharing their stories, survivors have the ability to not only transform their own lives but also to inspire others to join the fight against injustice. They ignite a collective spirit of resilience and hope, showing fellow survivors that their experiences matter and that change is possible. Survivors' narratives serve as a powerful reminder that each voice has the potential to create lasting impact, leading to a future where justice prevails.

As we continue our exploration into the far-reaching consequences of survivors sharing their stories, it is essential that we honor their narratives and create spaces that center their experiences. By amplifying their voices, incorporating their insights into policy-making processes, and supporting their healing journey, we can collectively strive towards a society that is more just, equitable, and compassionate.

Survivors and advocacy groups stand united in their mission to uncover the truth behind injustice. Through their collaboration, the seeds of change are sown, taking root and growing into a movement that defies the boundaries of silence and apathy. Let us listen, learn, and stand shoulder to shoulder with survivors as they rise, their stories illuminating the path to a world devoid of injustice.

Advocacy for Change

An in-depth look at the key role advocacy groups play in fighting for survivor rights and dismantling systems of injustice.

Advocacy groups have long been at the forefront of fighting for the rights of survivors and dismantling systems of injustice. They serve as the voice and driving force behind change, tirelessly advocating for the rights and support survivors deserve. In this chapter, we will delve into the world of advocacy groups, exploring their strategies, challenges, and the impact they have on survivors and society as a whole.

One of the essential roles that advocacy groups play is to raise awareness about the issues faced by survivors. They shed light on the often hidden realities of survivors' experiences, challenging societal perceptions and assumptions. By sharing survivors' stories and struggles, advocacy groups give a human face to the issue, fostering empathy and understanding among the general public.

But advocacy is not limited to simply raising awareness. These groups also actively engage in legislative and policy advocacy, working to bring about systemic changes that protect and empower survivors. They lobby for stronger laws, policies, and protocols that address the needs of survivors and hold perpetrators accountable. Through their tireless efforts, they strive to create an environment where survivors can seek justice and find the support they need to heal and rebuild their lives.

In addition to legislative advocacy, advocacy groups provide crucial support services to survivors. They offer a safe space for survivors to share their experiences, access resources, and connect with others who have faced similar challenges. Support groups, counseling services, and helplines are just a few examples of the valuable services provided by these organizations. By offering a comprehensive support network, advocacy groups ensure that survivors have the tools they need to navigate their healing journey.

Collaboration is a cornerstone of advocacy work. Advocacy groups often form alliances and coalitions, joining forces with other organizations that share their goals and values. By working together, these groups can amplify their impact, pool resources, and advocate for change on a larger scale. Collaborative efforts enable advocacy groups to reach more survivors, influence public opinion, and push for reforms that dismantle unjust systems.

It is important to acknowledge the challenges faced by advocacy groups in their pursuit of justice. They often operate in resource-limited environments, relying on limited funding and volunteer support to carry out their essential work. Navigating bureaucratic systems, facing opposition from powerful entities, and countering societal norms can be daunting tasks. Nonetheless, their unwavering commitment and dedication to a more just society keep them resilient and persistent.

As survivors and advocacy groups continue to face these challenges head-on, progress is being made. The collective efforts of these groups have led to significant policy reforms, changes in public perception, and increased support for survivors. However, there is still much work to be done. The fight for survivor rights and dismantling systems of injustice is an ongoing journey, requiring the sustained commitment and collaboration of advocacy groups, survivors, and society.

In the second half of this chapter, we will explore specific advocacy campaigns, success stories, and the future of survivor rights. But for now, we leave you with these words: advocacy groups are beacons of hope, guiding survivors towards a future where their rights are recognized, their voices are heard, and their healing is prioritized.

In the second half of this chapter, we will delve into specific advocacy campaigns that have been instrumental in bringing about positive change and elevating the voices of survivors. These campaigns have tackled critical issues, shed light on hidden injustices, and inspired collective action.

One impactful campaign that deserves recognition is the #MeToo movement. Originating as a social media hashtag in 2017, it quickly evolved into a global phenomenon, sparking conversations about sexual harassment and assault. Survivors, empowered by the movement, came forward and shared their stories, exposing the magnitude of the problem. Advocacy groups played a crucial role in supporting survivors who chose to disclose their experiences, providing them with assistance, resources, and a sense of solidarity. The #MeToo movement not only raised awareness but also contributed to policy changes and the creation of support networks for survivors.

Another notable campaign is the fight to end domestic violence. Advocacy groups have tirelessly worked to challenge societal norms that perpetuate this form of abuse. By conducting awareness campaigns, lobbying for stronger laws, and advocating for comprehensive support services, these groups have made significant strides. Their efforts have not only given survivors the courage to break the cycle of violence but have also led to improved legal protections and the establishment of shelters and counseling centers.

Furthermore, advocacy campaigns have emerged to tackle issues specific to marginalized communities. For example, organizations have been at the forefront of fighting for justice for Indigenous survivors of sexual violence. These campaigns highlight the unique challenges faced by Indigenous communities and advocate for culturally sensitive support programs, policy reforms, and initiatives aimed at dismantling the systemic barriers they face.

Success stories abound when it comes to advocacy campaigns. They serve as reminders of what can be achieved when survivors and advocacy groups come together and challenge the status quo. From securing landmark legal victories and amendments to the establishment of survivor-centered services, these successes demonstrate the transformative power of advocacy.

Looking to the future, the fight for survivor rights and dismantling systems of injustice requires continued dedication and collaboration. Advocacy groups must persist in holding institutions accountable for the failures that perpetuate injustice. They must continue to challenge the societal stigma surrounding survivors and work towards fostering a culture of empathy, understanding, and support.

To enhance their impact, advocacy groups can leverage the power of technology and social media, reaching wider audiences and mobilizing communities for change. With innovative campaigns, utilizing multimedia platforms to share survivors' stories, advocacy groups can create a groundswell of support and encourage meaningful dialogue.

In conclusion, advocacy groups have played a vital role in championing survivor rights and dismantling systems of injustice. Their unwavering commitment, collaboration, and resilience have led to significant milestones, shifting societal perceptions, and creating positive changes that benefit survivors and society as a whole. However, the journey is far from over, and continued efforts are necessary to ensure a future where survivor rights are recognized, voices are heard, and healing is prioritized.

Together, survivors, advocacy groups, and society must remain steadfast in their resolve to build a more just world, free from injustice and inequality. It is through collective action and ongoing advocacy that we can rise above the challenges, unite in our shared vision, and create lasting change.

Addressing Trauma

Trauma is a deeply distressing and often life-altering experience that can have profound impacts on an individual's mental and emotional well-being. Survivors of trauma often find themselves grappling with a range of complex emotions, disrupted thought patterns, and the profound effects it has on their lives. In this chapter, we aim to delve into the effects of trauma on survivors' mental and emotional well-being, as well as provide strategies for healing and recovery.

When trauma occurs, whether it is due to violence, abuse, or a catastrophic event, it can leave survivors feeling overwhelmed and emotionally shattered. The immediate aftermath often involves a range of intense reactions, including shock, disbelief, anger, fear, and confusion. These emotions, while overwhelming, are normal responses to abnormal circumstances.

In the long term, trauma can lead to the development of mental health conditions such as post-traumatic stress disorder (PTSD), depression, anxiety disorders, and substance abuse. Survivors may experience intrusive thoughts, flashbacks, nightmares, or a persistent sense of danger, making it difficult for them to trust others or feel safe in their surroundings. Furthermore, trauma can disrupt one's ability to maintain healthy relationships and can impact various aspects of daily life, including work, education, and overall functioning.

Acknowledging and addressing trauma is crucial for survivors' healing and recovery. The first step is to recognize the impact trauma has had on their lives and to validate their feelings and experiences. This validation can come from seeking support through therapy, joining support groups, or confiding in trusted friends or family members. Connecting with others who have gone through similar experiences can be immensely comforting, as survivors can find solace and understanding in knowing they are not alone.

The process of healing from trauma varies for each individual. However, it often involves finding healthy coping mechanisms and building resilience. Engaging in self-care activities such as exercise, practicing mindfulness or meditation, and engaging in creative outlets can help survivors manage their emotions and reduce stress. Additionally, seeking professional help from trauma-informed therapists can provide survivors with the tools and strategies necessary for their recovery journey.

Journaling can also be a powerful tool in processing trauma. Writing down one's thoughts and feelings can provide a sense of release and clarity, enabling survivors to make sense of their experiences. This process of introspection and reflection can pave the way for personal growth and empowerment.

As we navigate the terrain of trauma, it is essential to address the unique needs of survivors. Cultivating a safe and supportive environment where survivors feel heard and understood is paramount. Advocacy groups play a crucial role in amplifying their voices, shining a light on the injustice they have faced, and creating a platform for survivor-led movements for change.

In the second half of this chapter, we will explore additional strategies for healing and recovery, delving deeper into the role of therapy, the power of resilience, and the importance of fostering a supportive network. By unraveling the layers of trauma and understanding its impact, survivors can embark on a journey of healing, resilience, and ultimately, reclaiming their lives.

In the second half of this chapter, we will delve deeper into the strategies that can aid survivors in their healing and recovery journey. We will explore the pivotal role of therapy, the power of resilience, and the importance of fostering a supportive network.

Therapy is a crucial component of healing from trauma, as it provides survivors with a safe space to process their experiences, emotions, and thoughts. Trauma-informed therapists specialize in understanding the unique challenges faced by survivors and can provide guidance in navigating the path to recovery. Through various therapeutic techniques such as cognitive-behavioral therapy (CBT), eye movement desensitization and reprocessing (EMDR), and somatic experiencing, survivors can acquire the necessary tools to cope with their trauma and develop resilience.

CBT helps survivors challenge and reframe negative thought patterns that may have developed as a result of their traumatic experiences. By identifying and addressing these maladaptive thoughts, survivors can cultivate healthier beliefs about themselves and their place in the world. EMDR, on the other hand, focuses on reprocessing traumatic memories through guided eye movements or other bilateral stimulation. This technique can help lessen the emotional distress associated with the trauma, allowing survivors to integrate the experience into their past rather than their present.

Somatic experiencing recognizes that trauma not only affects the mind but also manifests in the body. This therapeutic approach emphasizes the release and regulation of physical sensations and impulses associated with trauma, promoting a greater sense of embodiment and resilience. Through a combination of these and other evidence-based therapeutic methods, survivors can gradually regain control over their lives and develop healthier coping mechanisms.

In addition to therapy, building resilience is an essential aspect of healing from trauma. Resilience is the ability to bounce back from adversity and to adapt positively to challenging circumstances. Survivors possess an innate strength and resourcefulness that can be nurtured and developed through various practices.

One such practice is cultivating self-compassion. Trauma can often lead survivors to blame themselves or feel an overwhelming sense of shame. By practicing self-compassion, survivors can learn to treat themselves with kindness, understanding, and acceptance. This involves acknowledging their pain without judgment and offering themselves the same compassion they would extend to a loved one in a similar situation.

Mindfulness is another powerful tool for building resilience. Engaging in mindfulness practices such as meditation, deep breathing exercises, or grounding techniques can help survivors stay present and centered. Mindfulness allows survivors to observe their thoughts and emotions without becoming overwhelmed by them, fostering a sense of control and inner peace.

Finding support from a network of understanding individuals is also crucial for survivors' healing and recovery. Connecting with other survivors, joining support groups, or engaging with advocacy organizations can provide survivors with a sense of belonging and validation. Sharing their stories in a safe and supportive environment not only helps survivors process and heal but also empowers them to become agents of change in combating injustice.

Survivors and advocacy groups play an instrumental role in raising awareness about trauma and highlighting the need for justice and support. By speaking out and sharing their stories, survivors can inspire others and create a ripple effect of healing, resilience, and social change.

As we conclude this chapter, it is important for survivors to remember that healing takes time and that their journey is unique. There is no right or wrong way to heal, and each survivor must find what works best for them. By acknowledging their trauma, seeking professional help, and embracing the power of resilience and support, survivors can reclaim their lives and move forward with hope, strength, and a renewed sense of purpose.

Together, survivors and advocacy groups can continue to rise against injustice, unveiling the truth behind the trauma they have endured, and paving the way for a brighter future for all.

Intersectionality Matters

An exploration of how intersecting identities, such as race, gender, class, and sexuality, can compound the injustices survivors face and the need for inclusive advocacy.

In a world where injustice is prevalent, survivors of various forms of discrimination and violence often face compounded adversities due to their intersecting identities. The concept of intersectionality, coined by legal scholar Kimberlé Crenshaw, sheds light on the complex layers of oppression experienced by individuals with multiple marginalized identities. This theoretical framework provides a deeper understanding of how race, gender, class, and sexuality intersect to create unique challenges for survivors, emphasizing the urgent need for inclusive advocacy.

When we examine the experiences of survivors, it becomes evident that the impact of their identities is not isolated but instead intertwines with their journey to healing and justice. Take, for example, Sophia, a survivor of domestic violence and racial discrimination. As a woman of color, Sophia faces the interlocking oppressions of racism and sexism, which perpetuate the violence she experienced within her relationship. The stereotypes and biases she encounters in society can further hinder her access to justice, making her path towards healing even more arduous.

Survivors like Sophia are not alone. The intersectionality of identities plays a significant role in determining the care and support available to individuals within the system. For instance, a survivor who belongs to a marginalized racial or ethnic group may be less likely to receive adequate medical and psychological services due to systemic biases. Similarly, survivors who identify as LGBTQ+ may fear judgement or discrimination when seeking assistance, resulting in them being less likely to come forward and share their stories.

Moreover, the impact of intersecting identities extends beyond the individual survivor and permeates within advocacy groups themselves. Many organizations that aim to support survivors inadvertently perpetuate exclusivity by failing to recognize and address intersectionality adequately. By focusing solely on one aspect of a survivor's identity, such as gender, some advocacy groups inadvertently exclude or marginalize those who experience additional layers of oppression. Recognizing the importance of intersectionality is crucial for fostering inclusive support systems that truly meet the diverse needs of survivors.

Effective advocacy for survivors necessitates acknowledging and addressing the intersectionality of their experiences. This begins with understanding the unique, multi-faceted struggles that survivors face and how these struggles are shaped by their intersecting identities. By recognizing the intricate interplay between race, gender, class, and sexuality, advocates can better tailor their approaches to meet the diverse needs of survivors and dismantle the oppressive systems that perpetuate their suffering.

Creating inclusive systems of support for survivors requires a comprehensive approach that reflects the real and complex experiences of those who have endured injustice. By dismantling silos and embracing intersectionality, we create space for survivors of all backgrounds and identities to find solace and empowerment. It is only through this inclusive advocacy that we can begin to untangle the web of injustices survivors face and forge a path towards collective healing and justice.

Within the world of survivors and advocacy groups, the recognition and understanding of intersectionality is paramount in addressing the myriad forms of discrimination and violence that individuals face. As we delve deeper into the complexities of intersectionality, it becomes evident that inclusive advocacy is not merely a choice but a necessity to dismantle the systems that perpetuate injustice.

In examining the experiences of survivors, we must acknowledge that their identities are not separate entities but interconnected facets that shape their hardships and journeys to healing. For instance, let us consider Alex, a survivor who faces the intersecting identities of being transgender and living with a disability. Alex encounters unique challenges in accessing healthcare and support services due to transphobia, ableism, and cisnormative biases. The barriers they face highlight the urgent need for comprehensive and inclusive support systems that address the compounded adversities individuals with multiple marginalized identities endure.

It is crucial to acknowledge that marginalized survivors often face systemic discrimination and biases within healthcare and support services. For example, individuals from racial and ethnic minority backgrounds may encounter language or cultural barriers, further hindering their access to resources. Additionally, survivors from lower socioeconomic backgrounds may struggle with financial constraints that limit their ability to seek necessary assistance. By understanding the intersecting factors that impact survivors' access to care, advocates can work towards dismantling the systemic barriers that perpetuate injustice.

Advocacy groups must recognize the importance of intersectionality in their work. To truly support survivors, organizations should take an intersectional approach that addresses the diverse needs and experiences of all individuals. By adopting a comprehensive framework that considers race, gender, class, sexuality, disability, and other intersecting identities, advocacy groups can create inclusive support systems that help survivors navigate the complexities of their journeys.

In this pursuit of inclusive advocacy, it is vital that survivor narratives are centered and uplifted. By amplifying the voices of survivors from diverse backgrounds, we showcase the diverse range of experiences and challenges they face. This approach not only provides validation and solidarity but also helps challenge harmful stereotypes and biases that perpetuate discrimination. Survivors who belong to marginalized communities should have equal opportunities to share their stories, shaping the narrative around injustice and pushing for meaningful change.

Furthermore, it is crucial for advocacy groups to actively engage in anti-oppressive practices and continually examine their own biases and limitations. By addressing internal barriers, organizations can create safe spaces where survivors feel empowered to come forward and seek assistance. Effective advocacy necessitates ongoing education and self-reflection to challenge and dismantle oppressive systems at both individual and systemic levels.

In conclusion, intersectionality matters immensely in the fight against injustice faced by survivors. By recognizing and addressing the intricate web of intersecting identities, advocates can tailor their approaches to meet the complex and unique needs of survivors. Inclusive advocacy requires dismantling silos, challenging prejudice, and fostering collaboration across different communities and identities. Only through this collective effort can we create a society where survivors are truly heard, supported, and empowered on their journeys towards healing and justice.

Legal Battle for Justice

An overview of the legal challenges survivors encounter when seeking justice, including the importance of legal reforms and support.

When survivors of injustice embark on the journey to seek justice, they often find themselves faced with an array of legal challenges that can seem insurmountable. Navigating the legal system and advocating for their rights takes immense courage and resilience. In this chapter, we will explore the formidable road survivors encounter on their quest for justice, shedding light on the importance of legal reforms and support systems that are crucial to their success.

One of the first challenges survivors face is the burden of proof. In cases of injustice, where the evidence may be scarce or difficult to obtain, survivors must gather the necessary documentation and testimonies to build a compelling legal case. This process can be emotionally tumultuous as it forces survivors to relive painful experiences and confront their trauma head-on. However, despite these obstacles, evidence plays an indispensable role in holding perpetrators accountable and ensuring justice is served.

Additionally, survivors often grapple with the statute of limitations. In some jurisdictions, there are strict time limits for initiating legal action, and if survivors fail to act within this designated period, they may be barred from pursuing justice altogether. The arbitrary nature of these time constraints places an unjust burden on survivors, especially considering the complex psychological effects that trauma can have on memory and decision-making. Addressing these limitations and advocating for extended or abolished statutes of limitations is an essential part of legal reform to ensure survivors are not denied justice due to the passage of time.

Another significant challenge survivors encounter is the arduous court process. From the initial filing of a lawsuit to the actual trial, the legal battle can be lengthy and emotionally draining. Survivors are required to participate in various legal procedures, including depositions and cross-examinations, which may force them to recount their traumatic experiences repeatedly. The adversarial nature of the court system can further exacerbate survivors' trauma, often leaving them feeling re-victimized or silenced. Reforming court procedures and introducing trauma-informed practices can contribute greatly to making the legal process more survivor-centered and supportive.

However, the legal challenges faced by survivors extend beyond the courtroom. A lack of resources and financial means to hire legal representation can be a significant barrier to accessing justice. Legal fees, court costs, and associated expenses can quickly accumulate, deterring survivors from pursuing legal action. This financial disparity further perpetuates systemic inequalities, as survivors from marginalized communities or with limited resources may find themselves unable to fight for their rights. Initiatives aimed at providing free legal aid and support to survivors are essential in addressing this disparity and ensuring equal access to justice for all.

Moreover, survivors often encounter societal prejudices and biases that threaten their credibility and hinder their pursuit of justice. Victim-blaming and disbelief are pervasive, perpetuating a culture that disempowers survivors and allows perpetrators to evade accountability. Challenging these harmful narratives and promoting empathy and understanding is crucial to dismantle the barriers survivors face within the legal system. By educating the public, raising awareness, and challenging societal norms, we can foster an environment that uplifts survivors and validates their experiences.

As we delve deeper into the challenges faced by survivors on their journey for justice, it becomes evident that legal reforms and support systems play an instrumental role in addressing these barriers. In the second half of this chapter, we will explore the transformative potential of legal advocacy groups and organizations dedicated to empowering survivors and enacting change. Through their tireless efforts, survivors find the strength and support they need to combat injustice. Join us as we uncover the incredible stories of resilience and triumph in the face of legal battles that these survivors navigate.As we delve deeper into the challenges faced by survivors on their journey for justice, it becomes evident that legal reforms and support systems play an instrumental role in addressing these barriers. In the second half of this chapter, we will explore the transformative potential of legal advocacy groups and organizations dedicated to empowering survivors and enacting change. Through their tireless efforts, survivors find the strength and support they need to combat injustice. Join us as we uncover the incredible stories of resilience and triumph in the face of legal battles that these survivors navigate.

Legal advocacy groups and organizations dedicated to survivors' rights have emerged as beacons of hope in the fight against injustice. They offer vital support, guidance, and resources to survivors, helping them navigate the complex legal landscape. These groups provide a safe space where survivors can share their experiences, connect with others who have faced similar challenges, and find solace in the knowledge that they are not alone.

One significant aspect of these organizations is their commitment to raising awareness and education. By conducting workshops, seminars, and public campaigns, they work diligently to inform the public about the realities of injustice survivors face and challenge harmful stereotypes and prejudices. Through their efforts, they aim to cultivate a society that is more empathetic and understanding, where survivors are not met with skepticism but rather with compassion and belief.

Moreover, legal advocacy groups play a pivotal role in advocating for legislative changes and pushing for legal reforms. They actively engage with policymakers, lawmakers, and governmental bodies to highlight the shortcomings of the existing legal system and propose meaningful changes. These reform campaigns often focus on mitigating the burdens survivors face, such as amending or extending statutes of limitations, enhancing trauma-informed court processes, and ensuring access to free legal aid for those who cannot afford representation.

By lobbying for legal reforms, these organizations strive to create an environment where survivors can pursue justice without unnecessary hurdles and obstacles. They also work towards ensuring that survivors have access to the necessary resources and support systems throughout their legal journey. By partnering with pro bono lawyers or providing financial assistance, they help level the playing field and address the financial disparities that prevent many survivors from seeking justice.

Furthermore, legal advocacy groups provide comprehensive support to survivors throughout the legal process. They offer guidance on navigating the intricacies of filing a lawsuit, ensuring survivors are aware of their legal rights and options. These organizations often provide emotional support, counseling, and therapy to help survivors cope with the trauma and emotional toll that legal battles may bring.

Through their dedication and passion, legal advocacy groups empower survivors and amplify their voices. They provide platforms for survivors to share their stories, advocate for change, and inspire others who may be going through similar experiences. These organizations foster a sense of community and solidarity among survivors, reminding them that they are not alone in their pursuit of justice.

In conclusion, the legal challenges faced by survivors on their quest for justice are formidable. However, amidst these challenges, legal advocacy groups and organizations stand as powerful allies, providing support, resources, and an unwavering commitment to change. They work tirelessly to reform the legal system, raise awareness, and empower survivors to seek justice. By amplifying the voices of survivors, challenging harmful narratives, and promoting inclusivity, these groups contribute to a society that values and uplifts survivors. Together, we can continue to unveil the truth behind injustice and build a more equitable and compassionate world for all.

Healing through Collective Action

I n times of adversity and injustice, survivors often find solace and strength in coming together as a collective. The power of collective action and community support cannot be overstated when it comes to creating healing spaces for survivors. Throughout history, we have witnessed the transformative effects that unity and solidarity have had in overcoming injustice and paving the way for healing.

Survivors, by definition, have endured unimaginable pain and trauma. The healing process is complex, and it requires more than individual strength. It necessitates the understanding, empathy, and support of others who have walked a similar path. By joining forces, survivors can break the isolation often associated with their experiences and find a sense of belonging within a community that understands their struggles intimately.

Collective action plays a crucial role in creating awareness and demanding justice. Survivors and advocacy groups have consistently demonstrated their resilience and determination to effect change on a larger scale. By raising their voices collectively, survivors amplify their stories, ensuring they are heard by those in positions of power, the media, and society at large.

Within the context of healing, collective action provides survivors with a platform to share their experiences, both as a cathartic process and as a means to inspire others. By speaking out, survivors become agents of change, empowering others to break the cycle of silence and secrecy. Through this collective sharing of stories, survivors and advocacy groups can foster empathy, challenge societal norms, and dismantle the stigma surrounding trauma.

Moreover, collective action brings survivors together to provide support for one another. By uniting with others who have undergone similar ordeals, survivors find validation and validation, which are crucial aspects of the healing process. Communities that understand the unique challenges faced by survivors can offer genuine empathy, reassurance, and guidance. By engaging in mutual aid, survivors not only receive the support they need but also become sources of strength for others in their community.

In addition to emotional support, collective action paves the way for practical resources and tangible change. Survivors and advocacy groups often collaborate to establish safe spaces, counseling programs, and legal initiatives aimed at supporting survivors and ensuring justice is served. By pooling their resources and expertise, these community-driven efforts provide survivors with the tools they need to heal and reclaim their lives.

Collective action can also serve as a catalyst for broader societal change. When survivors and their allies come together, their united voices drive conversations and policy reform, pushing the boundaries of what is deemed acceptable in society. By shedding light on the injustices survivors face, collective action not only seeks accountability but also challenges the systems that perpetuate harmful norms and behaviors.

The power of collective action and community support in creating healing spaces for survivors cannot be overstated. As we delve further into this chapter, we will explore real-life examples that showcase the incredible impact of collective healing. Stay tuned for the second half of this chapter, where we will examine how survivors and advocacy groups have harnessed the strength of community to promote healing and initiate concrete change. Together, they rise above the injustices they have faced, unveiling a truth that will inspire and empower survivors everywhere.While the transformative power of collective action and community support is evident, the impact is perhaps best understood through examining real-life examples of successful healing spaces for survivors. These stories serve as a testament to the resilience and strength of survivors and advocacy groups, inspiring others to join the movement for change.

One exemplary initiative is the Survivor Support Network, an online platform that emerged as a safe space for survivors to connect, share their stories, and provide support to one another. The network operates on the belief that healing occurs through collective understanding, empathy, and validation. By fostering a sense of community, survivors find solace in knowing that they are not alone in their experiences.

Within the Survivor Support Network, survivors can access a range of resources, including virtual support groups, trauma-informed therapy, and legal advice tailored to their specific needs. The peer-led support groups facilitate healing through shared experiences and mutual aid, allowing survivors to process their trauma and gain insight from others who have walked a similar path.

Another inspiring example is the collaborative effort between survivors, healthcare professionals, and community organizations to establish Healing Haven, a physical space dedicated to survivor-centered care. Healing Haven offers a holistic approach to healing, incorporating various wellness practices such as therapy, yoga, art therapy, and meditation. By creating this inclusive space, survivors can explore different healing modalities and find what works best for them individually.

In addition to providing emotional and mental support, Healing Haven partners with legal professionals to offer survivors guidance through the legal processes associated with seeking justice. The collaboration between survivors, healthcare providers, and the legal community highlights the importance of collective action in bridging the gaps between various sectors, ultimately resulting in a comprehensive support system for survivors.

Notably, these healing spaces also prioritize intersectional approaches to support. Recognizing that survivors come from diverse backgrounds, Healing Haven and the Survivor Support Network actively strive to address the specific needs of marginalized communities. By acknowledging the unique challenges faced by survivors from different socio-economic, racial, ethnic, and cultural backgrounds, these spaces work towards dismantling systemic barriers and promoting inclusivity.

One such initiative within these healing spaces is the provision of language services and culturally sensitive resources. By making information and support accessible in multiple languages and considering the cultural nuances of survivors' experiences, they aim to ensure that all individuals, regardless of their background, feel seen and supported.

These real-life examples demonstrate the incredible impact of collective healing spaces. They not only highlight the breadth and depth of support available but also showcase the power survivors have to initiate change and reclaim their lives. The strength and resilience of survivors, coupled with the solidarity within their communities, pave the way for societal transformation and justice reform.

As survivors and advocacy groups continue to come together, their united voices amplify awareness, challenge harmful norms, and demand justice for survivors. By harnessing the strength of collective action and drawing inspiration from these examples, survivors and advocacy groups everywhere are empowered to rise above the injustices they have faced, unveiling the truth behind injustice and forging a path towards healing and change.

In conclusion, the healing journey for survivors is greatly enhanced by the power of collective action and community support. Through shared experiences, validation, and access to essential resources, survivors can find solace, strength, and the tools they need to heal and reclaim their lives. Together, survivors and advocacy groups have the capacity to challenge societal norms, drive conversations, and effect systemic change. By standing united, survivors rise, inspiring and empowering others to join the movement towards healing and justice.

Unveiling the Truth

An exploration of the truth behind some high-profile cases of injustice and how survivors' stories brought the truth to light.

In the journey towards justice, there lies an often-unseen path carved by the brave survivors who refuse to be silenced. These individuals find themselves facing a system that favors the powerful and the perpetrators, often leaving the victims in the shadows of doubt and despair. The stories of these survivors are as varied as the injustices they have endured, yet they share a common thread of bravery, resilience, and an unwavering pursuit of truth.

One such case that shook the world was the trial of Amanda Turner, a case that exposed the dark underbelly of the judicial system. With her unwavering determination, Amanda stood tall against all odds, shedding light on the institutional failures that perpetuate injustice. Her story reverberated through the hearts of survivors everywhere, igniting their hope for a fairer society.

At the heart of Amanda's journey was the reality that survivors often face a long and arduous battle for justice. For years, Amanda fought tirelessly to bring her perpetrators to trial, shattering the walls of skepticism and victim-blaming that surrounded her. Her story awakened a nation as survivors and advocacy groups rallied alongside her, demanding an end to the culture of silence and an acknowledgment of the truth.

Amanda's case was not unique. Time and again, survivors' stories have toppled the walls of secrecy and unveiled the truth. From high-profile cases that garnered international attention to the countless survivors whose stories go untold, each instance is a testament to the power of raising one's voice against injustice.

In the case of Michael Johnson, a survivor of police brutality, the truth unfolded against a backdrop of racial discrimination and systemic violence. His journey, like so many others, was wrought with obstacles and setbacks, but his unwavering commitment to exposing the truth propelled him forward. Through community organizing and grassroots movements, Michael's experience shed light on the larger issue at hand – the need for police reform and accountability.

The survivors who dare to speak up face not only a broken system but also a society often quick to dismiss their claims. They are forced to relive their trauma in painful detail, carrying the burden of proof in a world that doubts their every word. Yet, in their collective strength, survivors create a ripple effect, inspiring others to share their own stories and seek justice.

The advent of social media has also played a pivotal role in unveiling the truth. Survivors now harness the power of digital platforms to share their experiences, connecting with others in similar situations and amplifying their voices. Through hashtags, viral campaigns, and online communities, survivors and advocacy groups have created a virtual haven where their stories resonate and the truth finds solace.

In this first half of the chapter, we have explored the courage and resilience of survivors who have unraveled the truth behind injustices that grip our society. From Amanda Turner's battle against a flawed system to Michael Johnson's fight against police brutality, their stories remind us of the urgent need to stand in solidarity with survivors, to listen, and to demand change.

As we delve into the second half of this chapter, brace yourself for the revelations that lie ahead. The pursuit of truth is fraught with twists and turns, but the survivors' voices shall prevail, unlocking untold secrets and paving the way for justice to prevail. Strap in and prepare to witness the transformative power of survivors rising and the truth finally being unveiled.As we delve further into the second half of this chapter, the journey of survivors continues to unfold, uncovering more hidden truths and shedding light on the depth of injustice that permeates our society. These brave individuals have braved countless obstacles and fought against a system that often suppresses their voices. Their tenacity and unwavering pursuit of justice serve as a powerful inspiration for survivors and advocacy groups alike.

One such survivor whose story exemplifies the strength and resilience of those who rise against injustice is Jenna Lawson. Jenna's battle against workplace harassment and discrimination became a catalyst for change within her industry. With courage, she came forward to share her story, risking everything in the pursuit of justice.

Jenna's experience exposed the toxic culture that had thrived within her workplace for far too long. Her testimony resonated deeply with countless other survivors, prompting an outpouring of support. Advocacy groups joined forces, demanding accountability and systemic change. Through their collective action, companies were forced to address the pervasive issue of workplace harassment, implement stricter policies, and establish support systems for survivors.

In another remarkable case, David Ramirez became an emblem of resilience and determination in the face of institutional indifference. David, a survivor of sexual assault, fought against a system that dismissed his claims and demanded his silence. Refusing to be silenced, he turned to the court of public opinion, sharing his story with the world.

Through social media, David's story gained traction, reaching millions of people who were inspired by his bravery and enraged by the lack of accountability. The unprecedented support he received emboldened countless survivors to speak out against their own perpetrators, unearthing a web of interconnected injustices.

David's case, along with many others, highlighted the importance of changing societal attitudes that perpetuate victim-blaming and stigmatization. Survivors and advocacy groups tirelessly worked to shift the narrative, emphasizing the need for empathy, compassion, and a dismantling of the structures that perpetuate injustice.

The power of survivors uniting cannot be underestimated. Together, they have exposed corrupt systems, challenged societal norms, and empowered others to share their own stories. Collectively, survivors and advocacy groups have become unstoppable forces, driving change and demanding a more just future.

As we near the end of this chapter, the truth behind injustice stands unveiled in all its complexity and devastation. The bravery and resilience of survivors have unlocked long-kept secrets and brought the harsh realities into the light. Their voices have reverberated through society, sparking conversations, and inspiring action.

To survivors and advocacy groups seeking justice, this chapter serves as a testament to your strength and unwavering commitment. The struggles you face are not in vain. Your stories have the power to ignite change and dismantle the very systems that perpetuate injustice.

In the face of adversity, survivors rise, and the truth prevails. Together, we must continue to fight for justice, support survivors, and ensure that their voices are heard. Only then can we truly uncover the truth and create a society where justice reigns and survivors find solace, healing, and the recognition they deserve.

A Call to Action

I n the face of adversity and injustice, survivors have risen above their pain and found the strength to speak their truth. Their stories serve as a powerful reminder that change is possible and that we all have a role to play in creating a just and equitable society. This chapter serves as a call to action—a rallying cry for individuals, communities, and institutions to stand in solidarity with survivors and work towards a better future.

Survivors have faced unimaginable challenges, yet their resilience and determination have led to significant strides in dismantling systems that perpetuate injustice. Their voices have shattered the silence surrounding issues such as sexual assault, domestic violence, and discrimination, bringing these dark realities into the light. But the battle is far from over.

For survivors, healing can be a lifelong journey. It requires support, understanding, and compassion from those around them. As individuals, we can play a crucial role by believing survivors when they come forward with their experiences. We must listen without judgment, providing a safe and empathetic space for them to share their stories. By truly hearing survivors, we validate their experiences and send a powerful message: you are not alone, and your voice matters.

Communities also have a significant responsibility in supporting survivors and fostering a culture of inclusivity and safety. It takes a collective effort to challenge the societal norms that perpetuate injustice. This means educating ourselves and others about the impact of trauma and the importance of consent. It means holding abusers accountable and providing survivors with access to comprehensive support services. By creating spaces where survivors can thrive, communities send a clear message that they will not tolerate injustice in any form.

Institutions, too, have a duty to step up and address the systemic issues that perpetuate injustice. This includes law enforcement agencies, educational institutions, workplaces, and other organizations that shape our society. They must institute policies and practices that protect survivors and promote gender equality. Training programs should educate staff about trauma-informed care and prevention strategies, ensuring that survivors are met with professionalism and understanding.

Moreover, survivor advocacy groups play a vital role in amplifying the voices of survivors and effecting change. They provide crucial resources, including counseling, legal support, and community networks. These organizations often work tirelessly to push for legislative reforms and advocate for survivors' rights. By supporting these groups, we can contribute to their vital work and ensure that survivors have the support they need to heal and rebuild their lives.

The progress we have made is commendable, but there is still much work to be done. Survivors deserve justice, and a fully equitable society demands our collective commitment. It is up to each and every one of us to be allies, advocates, and agents of change. By joining forces, we can create a society where survivors are empowered, where their experiences are heard and valued, and where justice and equality prevail.

In the face of adversity and injustice, survivors have risen above their pain and found the strength to speak their truth. Their stories serve as a powerful reminder that change is possible and that we all have a role to play in creating a just and equitable society. This chapter serves as a call to action—a rallying cry for individuals, communities, and institutions to stand in solidarity with survivors and work towards a better future.

Survivors have faced unimaginable challenges, yet their resilience and determination have led to significant strides in dismantling systems that perpetuate injustice. Their voices have shattered the silence surrounding issues such as sexual assault, domestic violence, and discrimination, bringing these dark realities into the light. But the battle is far from over.

For survivors, healing can be a lifelong journey. It requires support, understanding, and compassion from those around them. As individuals, we can play a crucial role by believing survivors when they come forward with their experiences. We must listen without judgment, providing a safe and empathetic space for them to share their stories. By truly hearing survivors, we validate their experiences and send a powerful message: you are not alone, and your voice matters.

Communities also have a significant responsibility in supporting survivors and fostering a culture of inclusivity and safety. It takes a collective effort to challenge the societal norms that perpetuate injustice. This means educating ourselves and others about the impact of trauma and the importance of consent. It means holding abusers accountable and providing survivors with access to comprehensive support services. By creating spaces where survivors can thrive, communities send a clear message that they will not tolerate injustice in any form.

Institutions, too, have a duty to step up and address the systemic issues that perpetuate injustice. This includes law enforcement agencies, educational institutions, workplaces, and other organizations that shape our society. They must institute policies and practices that protect survivors and promote gender equality. Training programs should educate staff about trauma-informed care and prevention strategies, ensuring that survivors are met with professionalism and understanding.

Moreover, survivor advocacy groups play a vital role in amplifying the voices of survivors and effecting change. They provide crucial resources, including counseling, legal support, and community networks. These organizations often work tirelessly to push for legislative reforms and advocate for survivors' rights. By supporting these groups, we can contribute to their vital work and ensure that survivors have the support they need to heal and rebuild their lives.

While progress has been made, there is still much work to be done. Survivors deserve justice, and a fully equitable society demands our collective commitment. It is up to each and every one of us to be allies, advocates, and agents of change. By joining forces, we can create a society where survivors are empowered, where their experiences are heard and valued, and where justice and equality prevail.

Conclusion

In this journey towards justice, it is crucial to remember that we are not alone. Together, survivors, advocacy groups, and our allies are a formidable force. We have the power to reshape societal norms, dismantle oppressive systems, and create a future where no one suffers in silence. Let us continue to rise, hand in hand, to unveil the truth behind injustice and build a world that stands strong with survivors.

Bonus Page

"I'm always trying to find ways to help people that may be struggling in the dire economic times we're facing. Through my research I've found a solution that rewards you with worthwhile, valuable, monetary rewards each time you swipe your debit card, no matter where you swipe it or what you swipe it for - gas, groceries, utilities, clothes, entertainment, whatever. If you'd like to be rewarded with real spendable value every time you swipe your debit card, click the link below for more information."

Start Rewarding Yourself Today!

POWER
SAVINGS
AS BIG
AS YOUR FUTURE

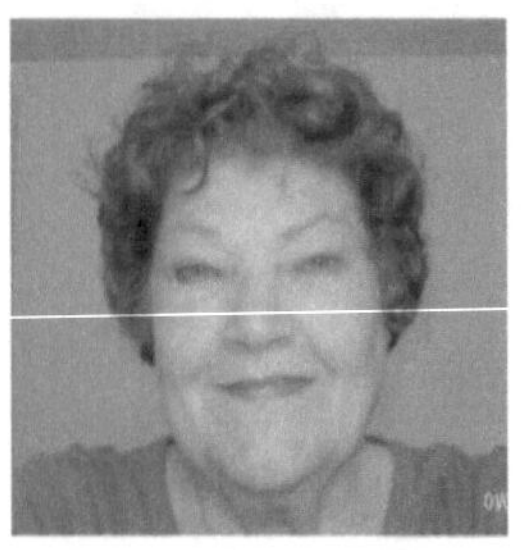

About the Author

Retired and living in beautiful Colorado for fifteen years now, and having time on my side, I've recently embarked on a new endeavor of internet marketing, which is a door-opening adventure for me, and is turning out to be more interesting every day, in terms of all the possibilities it has to offer. It allows the meeting of and collaborating with like-minded individuals who share some of the same ideas and goals, which is very enriching.

I'm also fairly new to authoring books, and with that comes a lot of satisfaction, and allows for new ideas and thoughts to be put onto paper, and into chapters.

You can connect with me on:

- https://soaringhi.tranzactcard.com
- http://twitter.com/hwyxchng
- https://www.facebook.com/CashinInOnline

Also by Wraydawn Shend

Would You Like to Design Your Home Like a Designer?

In this book you'll find Great Design & Decorating Ideas, that can be an inspiration to anyone, especially someone just entering the world of design. Possibilities are endless and Doors are opened to creative and intriguing ways for anyone to create their own Dream Home whatever their style and flair.Do you love the barn house style, eclectic, tropical, western vibe? Whatever style you love can be created, and your final achievement will be gratifying.

Interior Decorating:
Design & Decorating for Small Spaces

The AI Marketing Blueprint:

A Step-by-Step Guide for Network Marketing Leaders

Outlines how network marketing leaders can utilize AI to effectively identify and engage potential prospects, optimizing their efforts for maximum results.

Dives into the power of AI in tailoring marketing strategies precisely to individual prospects.

How Network Marketing Leaders Are Elevating Themselves with AI Technology

In an age where technology is redefining the way we conduct business, Network Marketing Leaders are at the forefront, harnessing the potential of Artificial Intelligence (AI) to revolutionize their strategies and elevate their performance. **This eBook delves deep into the integration of AI** in the network marketing sphere, showcasing how the industry's trailblazers are optimizing their outreach, targeting, and relationship-building with cutting-edge AI tools.

Has AI Diminished the Need for Ghost-writers?

This eBook navigates the history of ghost-writing, from its earliest days to its current prominence in the era of online influencers, celebrities, and business leaders. As it delves into the capacities of contemporary AI tools, readers will be introduced to the potentials and limitations of machine-generated content, analyzing if and how they match up to human-crafted narratives.

Echoes of Yesterday

From the depths of her horrifying, traumatic ordeal, a 15-year-old girl emerges as a pillar of strength and courage. Her journey through life had been one of pain, healing and justice. A life like a tapestry woven with threads of resilience. Through all her hardships, she chose to heal and grow stronger instead of letting them define her. She is living proof that even in the darkest of times, the human spirit can prevail.

Composting Made Simple: A Step-by-Step Guide for Beginners

Presenting endless possibilities for gardeners, farmers, environmentalists, and waste management professionals alike. Harnessing the power of composting paves the way toward a more sustainable, and resilient future where nature thrives, resources are conserved, and the planet is nourished.

Embracing New Beginnings

"Love Never Ages: A Grandmother's Journey of Redemption and Family" is a touching and inspiring tale that reminds us that love knows no age, and a grandmother's love can transcend any obstacle.

Join us on this heartwarming journey of a grandmother who found purpose, redemption, and the power to keep her family together.

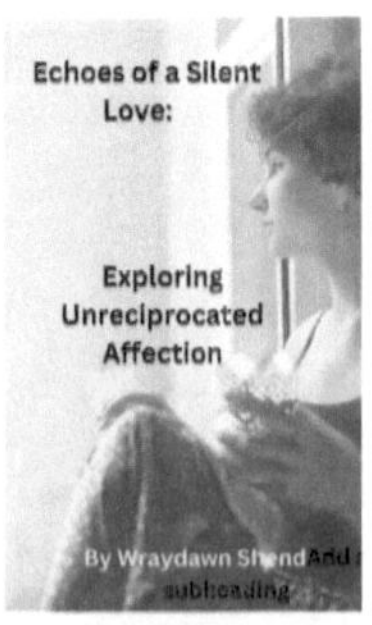

Echoes of a Silent Love: Exploring Unreciprocated Affection

Embark on a journey into the complex and often heart-wrenching world of unrequited love. This non-fiction book delves deep into the emotional landscape of what impact it can have on one's life when they have experienced the agonizing sting of affection that remains unreciprocated.